Michael McM[illegible] [illegible] in 1900, and grew up in Yorkshire. He studied Divinity at Aberdeen University for nine years, graduating with an Honours Degree in Divinity; followed by a Master's Degree, and then a Doctorate, in Historical Theology. He is an Associate Editor on Oxford's *New Dictionary of National Biography*. He presently acts also as a part-time tutor in the Divinity Faculty of Aberdeen University and also in the Centre for Continuing Education there.

Pauline Webb is a broadcaster and an accredited lay preacher in the Methodist Church. She is a Fellow of King's College, London, where she graduated in English Language and Literature, and also of the Selly Oak Colleges. She holds a Master's degree in Theology from Union Theological Seminary, New York and is a former Vice-Moderator of the World Council of Churches. Pauline is a co-editor of the *Dictionary of the Ecumenical Movement*.

HEARTS AFLAME

Prayers of Susanna,
John and Charles Wesley

Edited by

MICHAEL D. McMULLEN

TRi∆NGlE

First published 1995
Triangle
SPCK
Holy Trinity Church
Marylebone Road
London NW1 4DU

British Library Cataloguing in Publication Data
A catalogue record for this book is available from the British Library.
ISBN 0-281-04791-X

Typeset by Rowland Phototypesetting Ltd,
Bury St Edmunds, Suffolk
Printed in Great Britain by
BPC Paperbacks Ltd
Member of The British Printing Company Ltd

CONTENTS

—

I dedicate this book to my parents,
Patrick and June McMullen,
for their years of love
and self-sacrifice.

ACKNOWLEDGEMENTS

I should like to thank all those who have sought to help me in all that I do, but who have especially been a source of encouragement in the production of this book. My thanks go to the librarians at Wesley College, Bristol, for their assistance with Susanna's *Manuscripts*; to Liz for her helpful suggestions, and also her constant reading and re-reading of my work; to Evangeline and Zachary, for their inspiring faith that Daddy's book would soon be finished; and to Rachel Boulding, for her ongoing support and guidance.

FOREWORD

—

As one who travels a lot on ecumenical journeys, I have learned to travel lightly. Packing my case therefore places me in a dilemma. What books can I afford to include in my luggage alongside my Bible and the bulky documents which are always prescribed reading for conference proceedings? Eager to share with those of other traditions something of my own spiritual heritage I have always felt it essential to take with me two books. The first is *Hymns and Psalms*, which contains some of the best of Charles Wesley's theological and devotional verse. This poet of Methodism expresses in pristine simplicity both the fundamental doctrines of the whole catholic church and the personal experience of faith which kindled the flames of the Methodist revival. A hymn that has become universally loved uses this powerful image:

> O Thou who camest from above
> The pure celestial fire to impart
> Kindle a flame of sacred love
> On the mean altar of my heart

Devout Christians of every tradition would echo the prayer quoted in this present volume:

> Spirit of interceding grace,
> I know not how or what to pray,
> Assist my utter helplessness,
> The power into my heart convey.
> That God, acknowledging your groan,
> may answer in my prayers His own.

Beside the heavy tome of Charles Wesley's hymns, I carry too a less well-known book of John Wesley's prayers. In prose as concise and at times as sublime as his brother's poetry, he too takes us into that heart-warming experience which so inflamed an earnest, pious priest that he became a fervent and enthusiastic evangelist. The flavour of those prayers is caught in many of the following pages of this present book. Addressing God as his 'Covenant Friend', John anticipates that Covenant Service which was to become Methodism's unique contribution to the store of ecumenical liturgy:

> I give Thee my will.
> May I have no will of my own.
> Whatsoever Thou willest
> may I will and that only.
> May I will Thy glory
> in all things as Thou dost
> and make that my end in everything.

Now, thanks to the publication of *Hearts Aflame* I shall be able to replace my two volumes of poems and prayers with one slimmer handbook, which distils the essence of both Charles's and John's devotional writing, but brings the added bonus of revealing a treasure trove I have never stumbled on before. Here we are presented with the prayers of that remarkable woman who was the mother of these founders of Methodism, and whose own meditations were the inspiration of so much of what I had hitherto known only through the writings of her sons.

Like so many women, Susanna Wesley is remembered mainly through her relationship with others. She was the loyal wife of a rector who gained a certain notoriety because of his frequent debts, and she was the mother of nineteen children. Yet somehow in the midst of this hectic household she managed to find time and space for herself and her own spiritual needs. She devoted a large part of every day of her life to the nurture of her family. She drew up bye-laws for their education which were far in advance of the custom of the time. Children of the eighteenth century were expected to be seen and not heard. Susanna makes the remarkable claim that she managed to teach each of her children to 'cry quietly' by the end of the first year, so that 'the odious sound of children crying' was never heard in her household. Nevertheless she treated her children with respect and kindness. Her husband Samuel once remarked: 'I wonder at your patience: you have told that child twenty times the same thing.' Susanna calmly replied 'If I had satisfied myself by mentioning it only nineteen times I should have lost all my labour.'

To ensure the spiritual well-being of her family, Susanna allotted an hour each day to private conversation with each of her children separately, so that the ten who survived into adult life inherited a rich store of spiritual wisdom and personal counsel, which she continued to provide through continual correspondence after they had left home. Of John particularly she took special care. His rescue from the burning rectory at Epworth when he was still a small child convinced his mother that he was destined for some special purpose, as 'a brand plucked from the burning'. In response to her care, throughout his life he relied on her advice, which she always gave with what he described as 'a calm serenity'.

That serenity no doubt sprang from the fact that each day she also set aside time for herself and for her own devotional life. She was a woman of 'serious godliness' but also one who enjoyed and meditated on the simple delights of life. She kept her mind alert through extensive reading. This demanding blend of an active and contemplative life finds expression within her prayers. One can almost hear within them the constant interruptions which threaten the peace of any household. In her prayer 'Setting the Mind on Heaven' she reflects, with some frustration, on how difficult it is for a busy mother to pray, even on the Lord's day:

Another blessed day!
Lord, how could we support the cares and pains of life were it not for the refreshments of Thy dear and holy Day. How often do unforeseen accidents, indispositions and company

divert the thoughts, alienate the affections and strongly turn
aside the mind from intending and pursuing its eternal happiness!
Lord, might Thy creature remonstrate with Thy infinite
Majesty,
I would humbly beseech Thee to discover unto me the cause
why I so long labour under such and so many difficulties in
my way to Heaven,
as make me often of despairing ever to arrive there.

The prayers show an aspect of Susanna's life which is not so
well known as her domesticity. Not only was she a skilled
housewife, she was also a thoughtful and questioning
theologian, a disciplined writer and a fluent linguist. The
extracts from her *Devotional Journal* quoted in this book
do not shirk the larger questions of faith and doubt.
Though she is often concerned with self-examination,
there are some magnificent paeans of praise in sheer
wonder at the greatness and goodness of God. From one
who by all accounts had a hard life, beset by frequent illness
and tragedy, she yet manages to write prayers that meet
every circumstance of life with a glad response of faith.
Prayers such as the one entitled 'God's Happy Day' have a
poignant power:

> You did not give us being
> to increase your own happiness and glory,
> but to communicate Your happiness and glory.

Susanna's prayers communicate that happiness to us across
the centuries, calling us with her to rise above the chores of
our daily life into the unending delights of eternity. For
recovering these hitherto unpublished gems from ob-
scurity, Michael McMullen will earn not only the gratitude
of the people called Methodists but the appreciation of all
women and men who long to learn how to pray in the midst
of their busy lives.

Pauline Webb

The eighteenth century could be described as an age of cynicism fostering a spirit of indifference, at least as far as 'True Religion' was concerned. The Church of England, in the sad state that it was in at the time, was certainly not going to be the answer. Personal, living faith was not an issue: it just did not matter. Instead, dead morality was the stuff of sermons.

In the midst of this, God touched a handful of his servants in a special way, and thus the flame of the Evangelical Revival was lit. God granted great success to travelling preachers as they once again called sinners to repentance and to a personal faith in Christ. Both John Wesley and his brother, Charles, held key leadership positions in the Revival.

However, it was not from a void that these two men emerged. The influence of their remarkable mother, Susanna, on their lives and ministries is incalculable. This book consists of a selection of prayers taken from the writings of three particular members of the Wesley family: Susanna, John, and Charles.

It was suggested in W. L. Doughty's 1956 collection of Susanna's prayers that Susanna's name would be familiar to most people of cultured interests. This comment was made not only because she was the mother of Charles and John Wesley, but also on her own account too. She was a woman with a wide breadth of understanding, keen intellectual sympathies, and deep religious convictions. Sadly, today one suspects that the name of Susanna Wesley has become as neglected as the names of many other Christian giants.

This seems such a tragedy when one becomes aware of the living, vital relationship that Susanna had with God, and of the priceless, written legacy that she has left to the church. Her original writings, which have been consulted in the preparation of this volume, consist mainly of entries she made in her *Devotional Journal* in the early part of the eighteenth century.

From an early age, Susanna resolved to spend part of each day in personal communion with God. This usually consisted of devotions for one hour morning and evening. One finds from her *Journal* that she kept her resolution faithfully, even adding the noonday to her time spent alone with God.

Susanna sometimes recorded the results of her frequent communing with God in the form of the meditations already mentioned. As she herself records on the title page of one of the *Manuscripts*, they are the reflections and meditations of her heart as she communed with her God. They are the outpourings of a soul as it bathed in the presence of its Redeemer, as it rejoiced in the love of its Lord.

As we read in one of her meditations ('Prayer', p. 93), prayer is very precious, in that it is the immediate approach of a soul into God's presence. As such, she says, it should not be entered into lightly. For Susanna, it was an honour to speak to the Sovereign Lord of the universe. God was too great to be trifled with; too wise to be fooled by insincere devotion, a sacrifice without a heart. The only protection against cold and formal performances, Susanna realizes, is to commune regularly and constantly with God.

We learn from Clarke's *Memoirs* of the family that Susanna read widely, and though she endeavoured to conceal much of her extensive knowledge, it is felt to great advantage in all her writings. We learn of Susanna, for example, that early in her life she not only learned Latin, Greek, and French, but also became fluent in these languages.

As for her religion, it was as rational as it was scriptural and profound. In forming her creed, Susanna dug deep and laid her foundation upon a rock, and the storms and adversities of life never shook it. Even though she said that she did not despise or neglect the light of reason, speculative knowledge for its own sake was not the type of knowledge she desired.

To share in her own personal devotions is a great, but humbling, privilege. In her prayers, one experiences something of the majesty of God, his transcendence, and his love for mankind, as well as something of the life and character of Susanna, and the great pressures that she lived and worked under. I have taken the words as she wrote them, and, with very little change, have presented them – together with those of John and Charles – as prayers and reflections that can be used in both private and public devotions.

Susanna's maiden name was Annesley, daughter of Dr Samuel Annesley, a famous dissenter. She was born on 20 January 1669. At the age of twenty, she married the Revd Samuel Wesley, a committed Anglican. Samuel graduated with a BA from Oxford in 1688; was ordained priest in 1690; and became the rector at Epworth in 1695.

During the course of their marriage, the couple produced nineteen children, two of the most famous being John and Charles. Samuel was inept at financial management – even spending time in prison for debt – and therefore the resulting stresses upon Susanna were often very great. Also, Samuel was not altogether popular as a preacher, and it is even possible that the fire that destroyed the Wesleys' Epworth home was arson rather than an accident. In addition, Susanna suffered from prolonged bouts of ill-health.

When one is aware of something of the life of Susanna, the prayers of this remarkable woman, with their over-flowing joy and wholehearted trust in God, become all the more real. They indeed testify to the great, all-encompassing vision she had of her Almighty Saviour, a vision that the church desperately needs to recapture today. To that end, these prayers are taken from her

Journal, that they might be prayed and believed again.

As far as John is concerned, he was born some four years earlier than his brother Charles, in 1703, the fifteenth child in his family. At the age of ten he went to Charterhouse School in Surrey, followed by University at Oxford. He was ordained Deacon in 1725, and the following year he was elected a Fellow at Lincoln College, Oxford.

The following year he graduated with an MA, and in 1728 he was ordained Presbyter. In May 1738, John recorded that God strangely warmed his heart in an evangelical conversion experience. The impact of that event had far-reaching consequences, as the Evangelical Revival and the rise of Methodism testify.

In his teaching at Lincoln College, Oxford, we discover that John's aim in his teaching was not only to produce scholars, but *Christian* scholars. To that end, he wrote prayers for them for each day of the week. The original *Collection* is made up of devotions gleaned and composed from a wide variety of sources, including Scripture, prayer books, and other popular devotional books of his time.

It is a remarkable fact that Wesley produced this *Collection* some five years before his heart was warmly touched by God. John did produce a second *Collection* later in his life, and this formed part of his *Collected Works*. John's intention for his first publication was that it might encourage those who read it to give their whole hearts and lives to God. This worthy aim is echoed in the selection of prayers in *Hearts Aflame*, which includes a number from Wesley's *Collection*.

The *Journal* of John Wesley reveals very quickly the fact that John was a man who lived in a constant attitude of prayer. His writings reflect the fact that his experience of God was close, joyful, and life-changing, and this comes across clearly in his prayers and devotions. In one of his prayers included here (p. 82), for example, John reminds us that it was by prayer, by our communion with God, that the life of God was preserved in the soul. Prayer is something that is as vital for the spiritual life as air is to the natural life. John would have all Christians know that all they do, even when eating and sleeping, is prayer, when we have no other object in mind than God's love and the desire to please him.

Thus John Wesley's Christianity consisted of a deep and personal relationship with his loving, heavenly Father; and this was a relationship that John wanted as many as he could reach with the gospel to experience. This was the impetus behind John's miraculous record of preaching tours. It is calculated that throughout his ministry, John Wesley must have travelled 4,000 miles every year for over fifty years, covering in all some 250,000 miles, and preaching 40,000 sermons.

John's younger brother Charles was born in 1707, the eighteenth child of Samuel and Susanna. Charles also went to Oxford, and was ordained in 1735. Three years later, he – like John – experienced something of a conversion to a living, evangelical faith.

It appears that Charles may have inherited some of the talent that he possessed for hymn writing from his father, Samuel. It should come as little surprise to learn that Samuel also earned some degree of fame for his prose and poetic writings, even if it was in small measure compared to that of his son, Charles. Charles Wesley composed over seven thousand hymns and spiritual poems, many of which remain in constant use by the world-wide Church. We should not underestimate the enormous contribution hymn singing made to the success of the Evangelical Revival of the eighteenth century. Thus much of the credit must go directly to Charles Wesley.

Through such hymns as he and others wrote, ordinary people were able to sing of their new-found Christian experiences, while all the while imbibing biblical and spiritual truths. Charles wrote his hymns and spiritual poetry with the intention that they be used both in public praise and private devotion.

The selection reprinted here is taken from the multi-volume series entitled *The Poetical Works of John and Charles Wesley*. Charles's prayers, for that is what they truly are if prayer is the communing of the heart and soul with God, also tell us much about the man who composed them: a man filled with reverence for a holy, almighty, omniscient God; a man who knew what it was to have his spirit rise up in praise and adoration to a Being supremely worthy of all and more, and to whom he could return. He was also a man who knew that his God was the God who so loved humanity that he sent his own Divine Son to die for us all.

It is clear that Charles Wesley lived and breathed God's word. It permeates all that he wrote, and in his words one finds oneself constantly speaking, singing, and praying the written word of God. This is one of the reasons that make the words of Charles, as included in this book, so rich, so living and powerful, so vital and relevant. The other reason that his words are still among the most widely used in public and private devotion the world over is that they reflect the fact that they are the product of a heart and mind that are wholly committed to God. In his words, Charles Wesley reveals God to us afresh, as the infinite God who is far above all that we can imagine, and yet who, in Christ, has come to suffer to bring us back into fellowship with God.

However, this is not only the God of Charles Wesley; this is the God of his brother and of his mother. It is the God, too, of the Bible and the whole earth. It is to this living God that these prayers were originally prayed, and it is the aim of this book that Christians will once again utilize this part of their great and precious heritage and rejoice together in Christ.

I will end this preface with a prayer by John Wesley from his Preface to his 1733 *Collection*:

May He so enlighten our eyes, that we may reckon all things but loss, for the excellency of the knowledge of Christ Jesus our Lord; and so stablish our hearts that we may rejoice to suffer the loss of all things, and count them but Dung, that we may win Christ.

Dr Michael D. McMullen
Aberdeen, 1994

PRAYERS
IN SPECIAL TIMES

Joy – Trouble – Dealing in Business –
Confusion – Temptation – Evening Praise –
For the Night – Morning – Meals – Sabbath

INEXPRESSIBLE JOY

—

How I will blush Lord,
to behold that exceeding and eternal weight of glory,
that is conferred upon me for that little,
or rather nothing,
which I have done or suffered for you.

You gave me being, preserved me,
fed and cloathed me in my passage through the world;
and, what is infinitely more,
gave your only Son to die for me;
and have by your grace purified
and conducted me safe to your Glory.

Oh, blessed GRACE. Mysterious LOVE.
How shall I then adore and praise
what I cannot here apprehend aright.
How will love and joy work in the soul?
But I cannot express it, I cannot conceive it.

Susanna *Devotional Journal*

TRUE LOVE OF GOD

—

O God,
if to esteem and have the highest reverence for Thee;
if constantly and sincerely to acknowledge Thee,
the Supreme, the only desirable Good,
be to love Thee, I do love Thee!

If comparatively to despise and undervalue
all the world contains which is esteemed great, fair, or
     good;
if earnestly and constantly to desire Thee, Thy favour,
Thine acceptance, Thyself,
rather than any or all things Thou hast created,
be to love Thee, I do love Thee!

If to rejoice in Thine essential Majesty and Glory;
if to feel a vital joy overspread and cheer my heart
at each perception of Thy Blessedness,
at every thought that Thou art God
and that all things are in Thy power;
that there is none superior or equal to Thee,
be to Love Thee, I do love Thee.

Susanna Devotional Journal

GOD IS IN CONTROL

—

Lord, Nothing comes to pass
but by your appointment;
And you have a sovereign right
of disposing all persons and things
according as Your infinite wisdom shall determine.
Nor is it for a creature
to dispute the will of his Creator.
In all disappointments whatever,
in all the crosses and troubles
I meet with in this life
I must, therefore, submit with cheerfulness.

Susanna *Devotional Journal*

INVISIBLE YET PRESENT

—

Darkness and clouds around me roll,
but You shall in the clouds appear.
In this thick darkness of my soul
the great Invisible is near.

You now in Your pavilion dwell.
And when You do the veil remove
and when Your glory You reveal,
my fear shall all be lost in love.

Charles *Hymns and Poems*

IMITATING CHRIST

—

Lamb of God, I follow Thee,
willing as Thou art to be,
joyful in Thy steps to go,
suffering for Thy sake below.
Taking up my daily cross,
called to shame and pain and loss.
Well contented to sustain
All the rage of cruel men.

Jesus, in Thy gracious power,
lo I meet the fiery hour.
Calm, dispassionate, resigned,
armed with all Thy patient mind.
Turn, almighty as Thou art,
turn my persecutor's heart.
Let them to my faith be given,
let me meet my foes in heaven.

Charles *Hymns and Poems*

COUNTING THE COST

—

O Lord, help me to be wise and not take upon myself
the profession of a Christian,
without first considering the end of such a profession;
without weighing the difficulties I will encounter
in order to obtain that end.
The number and strength of my enemies, what my own
     powers are,
what succours I may expect and rely upon.

The end I seek is Thy glory, O God, and my own
     happiness.
Not the happiness of the body, but of the mind,
which is incapable of true happiness
till renewed and sanctified,
till restored to its native liberty,
till recovered from its lapse, and in all things
made conformable to Thy will and laws.

May happiness and purity hold just proportion to each
     other.
The difficulties are many and enemies very powerful.
But our Saviour hath said: 'Whoever will come after me,
let him deny himself, and take up his cross and follow
     me.'
Help me deny myself. I am my own worst enemy.

Susanna Devotional Journal

ALL THINGS DO WORK TOGETHER

—

O Lord, nothing can compare,
to the relief and satisfaction of mind
that results from the firm belief
that Thou dost govern the world.
I thank Thee too,
for the patience and resignation to Thy providence
that come as I reflect
that even the tumultuous and irregular actions
of sinful men are, nevertheless,
under Thy direction.

Thou art wise, good, and omnipotent,
and hath promised to make all things
work together for good to those that love Thee.
Since I must expect to meet with many difficulties,
much opposition, many disappointments
and daily trials of faith and patience
in my passage through this world,
let it be my highest wisdom to disengage my affections
as much as I lawfully may
from all transitory, temporal enjoyments.

That I might fix them on those more solid,
more rational and spiritual pleasures
which we are to enjoy
when we enter upon our state of immortality;
To endeavour to secure my eternal happiness
by using my utmost endeavours
to gain a treasure that lies beyond the reach
of all the storms and tempests of this world.
A kingdom that cannot be shaken by faction,
cannot be disturbed by ill men or ill angels,
where there are no parties or separate interests
to engage or divide men's affections,
but all shall most perfectly agree
to make up a Divine harmony of praise and adoration.

Susanna *Devotional Journal*

SUFFERING SERVANT

—

O Thou who wast despised and rejected of men,
when I am slighted by my friends,
disdained by my superiors,
overborne or ridiculed by my equals,
or contemptuously treated by my inferiors,
then let me cry out with Thy holy Martyr,
'It is now that I begin to be a disciple of Christ'.
Then let me thankfully accept and faithfully use
the happy occasion of improving
in Thy meek and lowly Spirit.

John *Collection of Prayers*

TIME FOR GOD

—

Deliver me, O God,
from too intense an application
to even necessary business.
I know how this dissipates my thoughts
from the one end of all my business,
and impairs that lively perception
I would ever retain of Thee
standing at my right hand.

I know the narrowness of my heart,
and that an eager attention to earthly things
leaves it no room for the things of heaven.
O teach me to go through all my employments
with so truly disengaged a heart
that I may still see Thee in all things,
and see Thee therein as continually looking upon me,
and searching my heart,
and that I may never impair that liberty of spirit
which is necessary for the love of Thee.

John *Collection of Prayers*

THE PROMISES OF GOD

—

O Lord, there is hardly a day that does not verify the
    truth of our Saviour's words,
'Sufficient to the day is the evil thereof.'
Through the weakness and corruptions of our nature,
the unavoidable business of our station,
many unforeseen accidents, unexpected company, cross
    occurrences,
with abundance of other things incident to human life,
we have occasion given us daily to exercise our virtues,
of one kind or other.

Yesterday Lord, Thou gavest me an extraordinary
    occasion to use
my justice and patience; today, my prudence,
    temperance, and charity, in forgiving injuries.
I did well in applying myself to the Supreme Fountain of
    virtue for grace in this perplexed affair;
and I accordingly succeeded well, and found that Thy
    strength is made perfect in weakness,
and that Thou art Truth itself, and all Thy promises are
    yes, and amen, through Jesus, our Mediator.

Susanna *Devotional Journal*

WORKING FOR GOD

—

Grant unto me blessed Lord, that great freedom of mind
that I might follow and attend on Jesus with a pure
 heart.
To be ever prepared and disposed to observe his example
and obey his precepts.

That I might manage the common affairs of life
so as not to misemploy or neglect
the improvement of my talents.
To be industrious without covetousness.
Diligent without anxiety.
To be as exact in each punctilio of action
as if success depended upon it.
Yet so resigned as to leave all events to Thee
and still attributing to Thee the praise of every good
 work.

Grant me that consummate prudence,
great purity, great separation from the world,
much liberty and a firm and steadfast faith
in the Lord Jesus, that will enable me to be accurate
in the common offices of life, yet at the same time
to use the world as though I had not used it.

Susanna Devotional Journal

LOOKING FORWARD

——

Pardon, good Lord, all my former sins,
and make me every day more zealous
and diligent to improve every opportunity
of building up my soul in Thy faith, love, and obedience.
Make Thyself always present to my mind,
and let Thy love fill and rule my soul in all those places,
companies, and employments, to which Thou callest me
    this day.

In all my passage through this world,
suffer not my heart to be set upon it,
but always fix my single eye and my undivided
    affections
on the prize of my high calling.
This one thing let me do:
let me so press towards this,
as to make all things else minister unto it;
and be careful so to use them,
as thereby to fit my soul for that pure bliss
which Thou hast prepared for those that love You.

John *Collection of Prayers*

THE BAFFLING MAZE

—

Do what You will, it should be so.
If now I cannot sound your mind,
Your work I shall hereafter know,
the meaning of Your conduct find.

Death shall unwind the baffling maze,
the impenetrable cloud remove.
And then I will see
that all Your ways were wisdom,
faithfulness and love.

Charles *Hymns and Poems*

TO THE ONLY WISE GOD

—

Were I permitted to choose a state of life,
or, positively to ask of You
anything in this world.
I would humbly choose,
and beg that I might be placed in such a station
wherein I might have daily bread with moderate care.
Without so much hurry and distraction
and that I might have more leisure
to retire from the world without injuring my
     dependants.

These are my present thoughts.
But yet, I do not know whether such a state
would really be best for me.
Nor am I assured that if I had more leisure,
I should be more zealously devoted to You, my God,
and serve You better than now.
Perhaps there might be as many temptations
in a quiet and private life
as there are in this.

Susanna Devotional Journal

GOD ANSWERS PRAYER

—

God hardly gives his Spirit even to those whom he has
    established in grace,
if they do not pray for it on all occasions,
not only once, but many times.
God does nothing but in answer to prayer;
and even they who have been converted to God without
    praying for it themselves (which is exceeding rare),
were not without the prayers of others.
Every new victory which a soul gains is the effect of a
    new prayer.

On every occasion of uneasiness,
we should retire to prayer,
that we may give place to the grace and light of God,
and then form our resolutions,
without being in any pain about what success they may
    have.
In the greatest temptations, a single look to Christ,
and the barely pronouncing His name,
suffice to overcome the wicked one so it be done with
    confidence and calmness of spirit.

John *Christian Perfection*

PRAYER IN TEMPTATION

—

Glory be to Thee, O Lord!
One step made towards virtue,
in that I find that whenever
there is any fervent prayer
against any particular, imminent,
or dangerous temptation,
the remembrance of that prayer
is a check upon the mind.

Nor dares it indulge a thought, a wish,
or an inclination so prayed against;
which is a great and strong proof
of an invisible Power
that does advert to our actions,
and hear our prayers,
and that is ever ready to assist
and keep such as sincerely,
though weakly, devote themselves to You.
Glory be to the sacred and ever blessed God,
Father, Son, and Holy Ghost!

Susanna *Devotional Journal*

A WELL-SPENT DAY

—

God, I give You the praise for days well spent.
But I am yet unsatisfied,
because I do not enjoy enough of You.
I apprehend myself at too great a distance from You.
I would have my soul more closely united to You
by faith and love.
You know Lord that I would love You above all things.

You made me, You know my desires, my expectations.
My joys all centre in You and it is You that I desire.
It is Your favour, Your acceptance, the communications
of Your grace that I earnestly wish for
more than anything in the world.

I rejoice in Your essential glory and blessedness.
I rejoice in my relation to You,
that You are my Father, my Lord and my God.
I thank You that You have brought me so far.
I will beware of despairing of Your mercy
for the time which is yet to come,
and will give You the glory of Your free grace.

Susanna *Devotional Journal*

THE WATCHING SHEPHERD

—

Thou Shepherd of Israel,
vouchsafe to receive me this night
and ever into Thy protection.
Accept my poor services,
and pardon the sinfulness of these
and all my holy duties.
Let it be Thy good pleasure
to put a period to sin and misery,
to infirmity and death,
and to hasten Thy Kingdom;
that we, with all that wait for Thy salvation,
may eternally love and praise Thee,
O God the Father, God the Son, and God the Holy
    Ghost,
throughout all ages, world without end.

John *Collection of Prayers*

GOD'S FATHERLY CARE

—

Continue Thy Fatherly care over us this night.
Preserve, defend, bless, and keep us,
that no evil may befall us
nor any plague come nigh our dwelling.
Give us comfortable sleep
to strengthen us for Thy service.
And for all that Jesus Christ hath done
and suffered for us,
to Thy Name, O blessed God of our salvation,
be the praise and honour and glory,
given by us and all Thy people,
now and for ever.

John *Collection of Prayers*

GOD'S MINISTERING ANGELS

—

Accept, O merciful Father,
my most humble thanks
for Thy preservation of me this day.
Continue Thy loving-kindness toward me,
and take me into Thy protection this night.
Let Thy holy angels watch over me
and defend me from evil men and evil spirits.
Let me rest in peace, and not sleep in sin,
and grant that I may rise more fit for Thy service.

John *Collection of Prayers*

GOD OUR DEFENDER

—

Accept our thanks
for Thy merciful preservation
of us all this day.
We are bold again to commit ourselves
unto Thee this night.
Defend us from all the powers of darkness;
and raise up our spirits,
together with our bodies,
in the morning to such a vigorous sense
of thy continual goodness,
as may provoke us all the day long
to an unwearied diligence in well-doing.

John *Collection of Prayers*

GOD'S HANDS

—

Into Thy hands we commend both our souls and bodies
which Thou hast mercifully preserved this day.
We trust in Thy watchful Providence
who givest Thy angels charge over us,
who art about our beds,
and about our paths,
and spiest out all our thoughts.

Continue these holy thoughts and desires in us
till we fall asleep,
that we may receive the light of morning
with a new joy in Thee
and thankful affection to Thee.

John *Collection of Prayers*

TAKE ALL MY DAYS

—

O Thou who dwellest in the light
which no man can approach,
in whose presence there is no night,
in the light of whose countenance
there is perpetual day,
I, Thy sinful servant,
whom Thou hast preserved this night,
who live by Thy power this day,
bless and glorify Thee,
for the defence of Thy almighty Providence,
and humbly pray Thee that this and all my days
may be wholly devoted to Thy service.

Send Thy Holy Spirit
to be the Guide of all my ways
and the Sanctifier of my soul and body.
Save, defend, and build me up in Thy fear and love.
Give unto me the light of Thy countenance,
peace from heaven,
and the salvation of my soul
in the day of the Lord Jesus.

John *Collection of Prayers*

WATCH OVER ME

—

Mercifully this day watch over me
with the eyes of Thy mercy.
Direct my soul and body
according to the rule of Thy will,
and fill my heart with Thy Holy Spirit,
that I may pass this day
and all the rest of my days to Thy glory.

John *Collection of Prayers*

LEAD ME

—

Preserve me from all those snares and temptations
which continually solicit me to offend Thee.
Guide me by Thy Holy Spirit in all those places
whither Thy Providence shall lead me this day,
and suffer not my communications with the world
to dissipate my thoughts,
to make me inadvertent to Thy presence
or luke warm in Thy service.
But let me always walk as in Thy sight,
and as one who knows this life
to be the seed-time of an eternal harvest.

John *Collection of Prayers*

BEGINNING THE DAY RIGHT

—

O that we could begin this day
in devout meditations,
in joy unspeakable,
and in blessing and praising Thee,
who hast given us such good hope
and everlasting consolation.

Lift up our minds
above all these little things below,
which are apt to distract our thoughts;
and keep them above
till our hearts are fully bent
to seek Thee every day,
in the way wherein Jesus hath gone before us.

John *Collection of Prayers*

GOD IS ALL WE NEED

—

Gracious Father, keep us, we pray Thee,
this day in Thy fear and favour,
and teach us, in all our thoughts, words and works,
to live to Thy glory.

If Thou guide us not, we go astray;
if Thou uphold us not, we fall.
Let Thy good providence be our defence,
and Thy good Spirit our guide and counsellor,
and supporter in all our ways.

And grant that we may do always what is acceptable in
    Thy sight,
through Jesus Christ our Lord,
in whose holy Name we close these our imperfect
    prayers.

John *Collection of Prayers*

GRACE BEFORE MEAT

—

O Lord, I beseech Thee,
give Thy blessing with what Thy mercy
has here provided me with,
that whether I eat or drink,
or whatsoever I do,
I may do all to Thy glory and praise,
through Jesus Christ my Lord.
Amen.

John *Collection of Prayers*

AFTER MEALS

—

O Lord my God,
bless Thy Holy Name for this mercy,
which I have now received
from Thy bounty and goodness.
Feed now my soul with Thy grace,
that I may make it my meat and drink
to do Thy gracious will,
through Jesus Christ my Saviour.
Amen.

John *Collection of Prayers*

GOD'S HAPPY DAY

—

Blessed be God for bringing me
to another of Your own most happy days.
The great business of the Day is Praise and Thanksgiving
and to the end that this may be devoutly performed.
I would spend some time contemplating
the essential perfections of Your Divine Nature
and when my soul is duly elevated
with those sublime and spiritual thoughts
then I would praise and adore You.

Blessed Being, You are the Creator
who made us out of nothing.
We are the effect of Your Infinite Power,
Wisdom and Goodness!
You had no need of us being perfectly happy.
You did not give us being
to increase Your own happiness and glory
but to communicate Your happiness and glory.
You are the Father of spirits and as such,
we owe You the honour and homage due from children.
We give You thanks for our creation.

Susanna *Devotional Journal*

THE DAY THE LORD HAS MADE

—

This is the Day that the Lord hath made I will rejoice
    and be glad therein.
Glory be to Thee Eternal Father of spirits
    for so kindly and mercifully indulging one Day in
    seven
to the souls Thou hast made.
Wherein it is their duty as well as happiness,
to retire from the business and hurry of a tumultuous
    and vexatious world,
and are permitted to enjoy a more immediate and
    uninterrupted attendance on the Divine Majesty.
Oh Blessed Indulgence! Oh most Happy Day!

Lord I can never sufficiently adore Thy Infinite Love and
    Goodness
in appropriating this seventh part of my time to Thy
    Self.
May these sacred moments ever be employed in Thy
    service.
May no vain unnecessary or unprofitable thoughts or
    discourse ever rob You of Your due honour and
    praise on this Day;
or deprive my soul of the peculiar advantages and
    blessings which are to be gained,
by the conscientious performance of the duties of the
    Day.

Susanna *Devotional Journal*

SETTING THE MIND ON HEAVEN

—

Another Blessed Day!
Lord how could we support the cares and pains of life
  were it not for the refreshments of Thy dear and
  holy Day!
Glory be to Thee, Oh Eternal, ever Blessed Goodness,
that hath in this probationary state,
afforded us such a vast invaluable blessing as a Sabbath
  is!
But oh how difficult a thing it is,
to preserve that devout and equal temper
that separation from the world and freedom from all
  worldly regards on this Blessed Day
which we so much desire and so often pray for!

How often do unforeseen accidents, indispositions and
  company divert the thoughts, alienate the
  affections,
and strongly turn aside the mind
from intending and pursuing its eternal happiness!
Lord might Thy creature remonstrate with Thy infinite
  Majesty,
I would humbly beseech Thee to discover unto me the
  cause,
why I so long labour under such and so many difficulties
  in my way to Heaven,
as make me often of despairing ever to arrive there.

Susanna *Devotional Journal*

PRAYERS
OF CHRISTIAN DEVOTION

Praise – Confession – Thanksgiving –
Devotion – Repentance – Hope –
Prayer – Dedication – Intercession –
For the Holy Spirit

PRAISE FOR THE INCARNATION

—

Praise the Lord O my soul
and all that is within me
bless His holy Name!
For ever adored and magnified
be the Eternal God,
by all Angels and men
for Your inconceivable purity
and boundless, incomprehensible Love to mankind.

Lord Jesus Christ
the Eternal Son of God
by an ineffable and incomprehensible generation;
who is one with the Father and Sacred Spirit;
equal to the Father as touching His Godhead;
and who therefore thought it no robbery
to take upon Himself the title of God,
this Christ, this Jesus, the Son of the Blessed,
assumed our nature;
took upon Himself the form of a Servant;
and was made of no reputation,
only that He might become the Saviour of the World.

And had You never gone further,
even this first step of condescension,
the veiling Your native Glory and Splendour
with our Humanity, without any personal suffering,
would have been so Stupendous, so amazing,
as might justly have exacted a tribute
of adoration and praise,
from the whole human nature,
for that exceeding abundant honour,
for that vast accession of Glory
which it reaches by that mysterious hypostatic union.

But O Lord,
when the thoughts proceed further
on this vast subject,
we see clearly the end for which the Son of God
took upon him our nature.
It was to suffer a lurid, painful, shameful death
that he might satisfy the Justice of God,
that he might purify and reinstate us
in the favour of God and purchase eternal salvation
for those that believe.

Susanna *Devotional Journal*

PRAISE TO THE SECOND ADAM

—

My God, all the power or capacity we have of attaining
    to the knowledge of God and ourselves,
all the right we have to the Tree of Life or Eternal Life,
is only on account of the Second Covenant made in and
    by the Lord Jesus;
who united His Divine Person, not to this or that
    particular man, but to the whole Human Nature.

For which reason He is called the Second Adam,
or Man in general, as the name Adam signifies.
That as in Adam all died, so in Christ,
all might be made alive.
It is in, or by the sin of the First Adam, that all men
    were brought into a state of Mortality,
in danger of an endless separation from You,
with all the dreadful consequences thereof.
So by the Second Adam,
all men are brought into a Salvable Condition;
may have the lapse of their nature cured and thereby
    become capable of enjoying Your Favour and
    Presence,
the effects of which is Life Eternal!

Susanna *Devotional Journal*

PRAISE TO THE TRINITY

—

Glory be to Thee, O most adorable Father,
who after Thou hadst finished the work of creation,
enteredst into Thy eternal rest.

Glory be to Thee, O holy Jesus,
who having through the eternal Spirit
offered Thyself a full, perfect, and sufficient sacrifice for
the sins of the whole world,
didst rise again the third day from the dead,
and hadst all power given Thee both in heaven and on
earth.

Glory be to Thee, O blessed Spirit,
who proceeding from the Father and the Son,
didst come down in fiery tongues on the Apostles,
on the first day of the week,
and didst enable them to preach the glad tidings of
salvation to a sinful world,
and has ever since been moving on the faces of men's
souls,
as Thou didst once on the face of the great deep,
bringing them out of that dark chaos in which they were
involved.

Glory be to Thee, O holy undivided Trinity,
for jointly concurring in the great work of our
    redemption,
and restoring us again to the glorious liberty of the sons
    of God.

Glory be to Thee, who in compassion to human
    weakness,
hast appointed a solemn day for the remembrance of Thy
    inestimable benefits.

John *Collection of Prayers*

THE NATURE OF GOD

—

Help me Almighty God,
to speak magnificently and worthily of You.
You are the high and lofty one
that inhabitest eternity,
the Creator of the universe.

You are immense, infinitely perfect mind.
Holiness is Your essence,
the eternal, infinite rectitude of Your nature.
You are absolutely separated
from all moral imperfection.
There is no contrariety or contradiction in You,
no variableness, neither shadow of turning.

You are power, wisdom, justice, goodness and truth!
You are perfection of being,
comprehending all and infinitely more
than we can possibly conceive.
You are essential glory.

Susanna *Devotional Journal*

GOD'S NAME

—

I know Lord,
that there is more significancy in Thy awful name
by which Thou condescended to manifest Thyself
to the Israelites, 'I am',
than can be comprehended or expressed
by any or all the words that are comprised
in all the languages of the earth.

Susanna *Devotional Journal*

GOD'S INEXHAUSTIBLE POWER

—

As Your Infinite, Almighty Power
was not exhausted in the creation of the universe,
nor could possibly be so, though You should create
        more,
but though You should still continue to create, ad
        infinitum,
Your essential goodness is the same,
so neither are the merits of Your passion,
exhausted by those that are actually redeemed;
but were there as many worlds to save as Omnipotence
        could create,
Your one sacrifice of Yourself would be sufficient to save
        them all.

Susanna *Devotional Journal*

GOD THE SUPREME GOOD

—

Lord you are Being itself.
The I Am, and therefore must necessarily be the
    Supreme Good.

You are so infinitely blessed,
that every perception of your blissful presence imparts a
    vital gladness to the heart.
Every degree of approach towards you is in the same
    proportion,
a degree of happiness.

I often think that were you always present to my mind,
as I am present to you, there would be no pain, nor sense
    of misery.
I have long since chosen you for my only Good,
my All, my Pleasure, my Happiness in this world,
as well as in the world to come.

Susanna Letters

THE PERFECTION OF GOD

—

Now if I consider the infinite,
boundless, incomprehensible Perfections of you the ever-
    blessed God,
I may easily conceive that evil, that sin,
is the greatest contradiction imaginable to your most
    holy Nature.

And that no evil, no disease, pain, or natural uncleanness
    whatever, is so hateful, so loathsome to us,
as the corruptions and imperfections of the soul are to
    you.

You are Infinite Purity,
absolutely separated from all mortal imperfection.
Your Divine Intellect is all brightness, all perfect.
It was never, and can never be capable of the least
    ignorance.

You are Truth,
nor can you be weary or indisposed
in contemplating that great attribute of your most
    perfect Nature,
but have a constant steady view of truth.

As you fully comprehend at once all things
past, present, and to come;
so all objects appear to you simple, naked,
undisguised in their natures, properties,
relations and ends, truly as they are.
Nor is it possible
that you should be guilty of error, or mistake;
of making any false judgement or wrong determination.

You are Goodness, and your most holy will cannot
     swerve,
or decline from what is so.
You always will what is absolutely best;
nor can you possibly be deceived or deceive any one.

The Ideas of your Divine mind are amiable,
clear, holy, just, good, and useful.
You are of purer eyes than to behold iniquity.
Your love and desire, though boundless,
immense and infinite, are yet regular, immutable,
always under the direction of your unerring Wisdom,
your unlimited Goodness, and your impartial Justice.

Who can by searching find out you?
Who can find you the Almighty to perfection?
What Angel is worthy to speak your praise,
who dwelleth in the inaccessible Height,
which no man can approach unto?

And though you are always surrounded by thousands,
and tens of thousands of those pure and happy spirits;
yet they are represented to us as veiling their faces,
as if conscious of too much imperfection and weakness
to behold your Glory.

And if you charged your Angels with folly,
and those stars are not pure in your sight;
how much less men that are worms,
and this son of man that is a worm?

Susanna *Devotional Journal*

GOD AS COVENANT-FRIEND

—

And now, glory be to you, O God the Father,
whom I shall be bold from this day forward
to look upon as my God and Father;
that ever you should find out such a way for recovery of
    undone Sinners.
Glory be to you, O God the Son, who have loved me,
and washed me from my sins in your own blood,
and are now become my Saviour and Redeemer.
Glory be to you, O God the Holy Ghost,
who by the Finger of your almighty power have turned
    about my heart from Sin to God.

O dreadful Jehovah, the Lord God Omnipotent,
Father, Son, and Holy Ghost,
you are now become my Covenant-Friend,
and I, through your infinite grace,
am become your Covenant-servant.

Amen. So be it. And the Covenant which I have made
    on earth,
let it be ratified in heaven.

John 'Covenant Service'

THE MIND OF JESUS

—

Plant and root and fix in me all the mind that was in
    you.
Settled peace I then shall find.
Jesu's is a quiet mind.

Then in the accursed lust of praise shall in me no more
    have place.
Pride no more my soul shall bind.
Jesu's is a humble mind.

I shall suffer and fulfil all my Father's gracious will.
Be in all alike resigned.
Jesu's is a patient mind.

When it's deeply rooted here, perfect love shall cast out
    fear.
Fear does servile spirits bind.
Jesu's is a noble mind.

When I feel it fixed within I shall triumph over sin.
How should sin an entrance find?
Jesu's is a spotless mind.

I shall nothing know beside Jesus and Him crucified.
I shall all to Him be joined.
Jesu's is a loving mind.

I shall fully be restored to the image of my Lord.
Witnessing to all mankind.
Jesu's is a perfect mind.

Charles Hymns and Poems

THE TRANSCENDENCE OF GOD

—

Almighty God,
I cannot tell what it is
to have a just sense of You
as Father, Son and Holy Spirit.
After so many years inquiry,
so long reading and so much thinking,
Your boundless essence appears more inexplicable,
the perfection of Your glory
more bright and inaccessible.

The farther I search, the less I discover.
I seem more ignorant now
than when I first began to know something of You.
I cannot do You the justice I would.
I cannot attain to an adequate notion of You,
a proper knowledge of Your essence.
Yet we may discover Your glory
in the creation of the world
and the redemption and regeneration
of the human nature.

Susanna *Devotional Journal*

PRAISE OF CREATION

—

Thou art praised, O Lord, by all Thy works,
and magnified by everything which Thou hast created.

The sun rejoiceth to run his course,
that he may set forth Thy praise who madest him.
Nor do the moon and stars refrain to manifest Thy
glory,
even amidst the silent night.

The earth breathes forth perfumes, as incense to Thee,
her sacred King.
Who hast crowned her with herbs and trees,
and beautified her with hills and dales.

The deep uttereth her voice, and lifteth up her hands on
high to Thee,
the great Creator, the universal King, the everlasting
God.

The floods clap their hands,
and the hills are joyful together before Thee.
The fruitful vales rejoice and sing Thy praise.

John *Collection of Prayers*

CREATION TESTIFIES TO GOD'S EXISTENCE

—

The Existence of all things or even of one particular
thing that hath a being,
whether it be in Heaven above,
or on the Earth beneath,
or in the waters under the Earth,
loudly proclaim Your Power, Wisdom and Goodness as
the Great Creator.

Just as by the sight of some noble Fabric,
or curious piece of Art,
we may justly infer that some wise Builder or cunning
Artificer has been at work.
So when we behold this goodly system of beings
we may reasonably conclude that there must necessarily
be some Self-Existent, Eternal Being,
by whose Almighty Power all things were created.
And this Being is God.

Susanna *Devotional Journal*

MEDITATION ON THE CREATOR AND
HIS CREATION

—

If all things were formed by chance at first,
how comes it to pass, that we see no such wonderful
    effects of chance now?
We now observe a fixed and unalterable Rule,
a certain admirable Method in the production of all
    things.

Did chance appoint the various seasons of the year?
The alternate vicissitudes of Day and Night?
What Almighty Power and Wisdom must we ascribe to
    this blind cause,
if we suppose it able to form the Heavenly Bodies,
those stupendous Globes of Light,
or to contrive their just positions and regular motions.

Does chance sustain the Earth, which hangs suspended
    like a Ball in the air?
Or did it bound the sea within certain limits,
and make its barriers of weak land which prevents it
    from overflowing the Earth
notwithstanding the impetuous violence of its waves?

Observe but the vegetable part of the world and tell me,
whether you think it was possible for chance to produce
  the admirable variety of Trees, Plants, Flowers and
  Herbs?
Can it be chance that causes the Earth to bring them
  forth in their seasons,
and inspires them with that spark of Life that is in them,
and disposes them to attract nourishment, to grow,
  increase and seminate,
for the preserving themselves, and their kind.
Not to mention their various virtues for food and
  medicine?

It is impossible to conceive this power in so stupid a
  cause,
especially if we consider that the most powerful, the
  most learned and wisest of men
are not able to create one single Blade of Grass,
nay nor so much as to understand and clearly decipher
  the great varieties in the production and process of
  its short,
yet wonderful contrivance.

Susanna Devotional Journal

ONLY GOD KNOWS WHAT GOD IS

—

Even if all the Angelic and Human Nature were united
    in One Mind,
it would fail in power to define Your Infinite Perfection!
GOD, ONLY YOU KNOW WHAT GOD IS!

Nor can You be said otherwise to comprehend Yourself,
than that nothing in Your Essence or Nature is hid from
    or unknown to You.
I must freely own, I am of all others the most unfit and
    unworthy to speak on this boundless subject!
I cannot so much as think of it,
but I feel my understanding confounded and
    overwhelmed with the least perception of Your
    Majesty and Glory!

I am never at so great a loss for words, as when I
    endeavour to express the little and imperfect sense I
    have of You.
I know but very little of my own Nature, how then shall
    I presume to speak of Yours that created all things!
That infinitely transcends our most sublime
    apprehensions!
Who dwelleth in inaccessible Light, unto which no man
    can approach!

Susanna *Devotional Journal*

WHO IS LIKE THE LORD?

———

God You are one pure Essence!
Fulness, Perfection of Being!
Self Existent, Necessary, Infinite, Eternal!

Comprehending in Your most Blessed nature, all the
    perfection a Spirit is capable of!
Such as Power, Wisdom, Justice, Goodness, Truth,
    Holiness, and Immutability.

You are whatever is Great or Good! Glory! Perfection in
    the Abstract!
Absolutely separated from all moral evil,
from whatever pollution can possibly defile a Spirit!
In a word You are Being itself!

Susanna *Devotional Journal*

THE REASON FOR PRAISE

—

O God,
what abundant reason I have to adore, to praise,
and to magnify Your goodness and love for sending Your
Son into the world to die for sinners.
What reason have I to praise, adore and love that
Saviour who suffered so much to redeem me from
that place of torment!
What sentiments of gratitude should I conceive for such
boundless charity to souls!

How gladly and cheerfully should I take up my cross for
You who suffered death upon the Cross for me.
Help me to praise and adore the blessed Spirit
Who sanctifies and illumines my mind;
Who cooperates with the means of grace;
and Who condescends to visit, assist and refresh my soul
by His powerful influences.
Glory be to the Father, Son, and Holy Ghost!
Joint Authors of my salvation!

Susanna *Devotional Journal*

THE PRODIGAL'S PRAYER

——

O Most dreadful God, for the passion of your Son,
I beseech you to accept of your poor Prodigal now
    prostrating himself at your door:
I have fallen from you by my Iniquity,
and am by nature a Son of Death,
and a thousandfold more the Child of Hell by my wicked
    practice;

But of your infinite grace you have promised mercy to
    me in Christ
if I will but turn to you with all my heart:
therefore upon the call of your Gospel,
I am now come in,
and throwing down my weapons, submit myself to your
    mercy.

Now, Almighty God, searcher of Hearts,
you know that I make this Covenant with you this day,
without any known guile or reservation, beseeching you,
if you espy any flaw or falsehood therein,
you would discover it to me, and help me to do it aright.

John 'Covenant Service'

FATHER OF MERCIES

—

May all my thoughts, words, and works tend to Thy
    glory.
Heal, O Father of mercies, all my infirmities;
strengthen me against all my follies;
and forgive me all my sins,
and let them not cry louder in Thine ears for vengeance,
than my prayers for mercy and forgiveness.

John *Collection of Prayers*

A CONTRITE SPIRIT

—

I desire to offer unto Thee, O Lord,
my evening sacrifice, the sacrifice of a contrite spirit.
Have mercy upon me, O God, after Thy great goodness;
and after the multitude of Thy mercies, do away mine
    offences.

Let Thy unspeakable mercy free me from the sins I have
    committed,
and deliver me from the punishment I have deserved.

O save me from every work of darkness and cleanse me
    from all filthiness of flesh and spirit,
that, for the time to come, I may, with a pure heart and
    mind, follow Thee, the only true God.

John *Collection of Prayers*

JESUS OUR ADVOCATE

—

O Lord, my Judge, Thou art also my Redeemer.
I have sinned, but Thou, O Blessed Jesus, art my
    Advocate.
Spare me, gracious Lord,
spare Thy servant whom Thou hast redeemed with Thy
    most precious blood.
Deliver me from the power of sin and preserve me from
    the punishment of it.

John *Collection of Prayers*

LORD HAVE MERCY

——

O God the Father,
who canst not be thought to have made me
only to destroy me,
> have mercy upon me.
O God the Son,
who knowing Thy Father's will,
didst come into the world to save me,
> have mercy upon me.
O God, the Holy Ghost,
who to the same end hast so often breathed
holy thoughts into me,
> have mercy upon me.
O Holy, Blessed, and Glorious Trinity,
whom in Three Persons, I adore as One God,
> have mercy upon me.

John *Collection of Prayers*

A THANKFUL HEART

—

Father of Lights,
from whom proceeds whatever all your creatures need.
Whose goodness providently nigh, feeds the young
    ravens when they cry.
To you I look.
My heart prepare.
Suggest, and hearken to my prayer.

Since by your light myself I see,
naked, and poor, and void of you.
Your eyes must all my thoughts survey,
preventing what my lips would say.
You see my wants, for help they call.
Before I speak you know them all.

You know the baseness of my mind.
Wayward, and impotent, and blind.
You know how unsubdued my will,
averse to good and prone to ill.
You know how wide my passions rove,
nor checked by fear,
nor charmed by love.

Fain would I know as known by you,
and feel the indigence I see.
Ah give me, Lord, I still would say,
a heart to mourn, a heart to pray.
My business this, my only care,
my Life, my every breath be prayer.

Father, I want a thankful heart.
I want to taste how good you are.
To plunge me in your mercy's sea
and comprehend your love to me.
The breadth, and length, and depth, and height,
of Love divinely infinite.

Father,
I long my soul to raise and dwell for ever on your praise.
Your praise with glorious joy to tell in ecstasy
     unspeakable.
While the full power of faith I know and reign
     triumphant here below.

Charles *Hymns and Poems*

THE GIFT OF THANKS

—

Hail, holy, heaven-ascended Child,
who God and man has reconciled,
whom angels bow before!
Whatever I have of good to give, to you,
from whom I first receive,
I thankfully restore.

To you my heart I open wide.
The myrrh of passions mortified,
the gold of charity,
the incense sweet of humble prayer,
I now, your prostrate worshipper
with joy present to you.

Charles *Hymns and Prayers*

FILLED WITH GOD

—

When we have received any favour from God,
we ought to retire, if not into our closets,
into our hearts, and say,
'I come, Lord,
to restore to you what you have given,
and I freely relinquish it,
to enter again into my own nothingness.'

For what is the most perfect creature in heaven or earth
    in your presence,
but a void capable of being filled with you and by you,
as the air which is void and dark is capable of being filled
    with the light of the sun,
who withdraws it every day to restore it the next,
there being nothing in the air that either appropriates
    this light or resists it.

O give me the same faculty of receiving and restoring
    your grace and good works!
I say yours, for I acknowledge the root from which they
    spring is in you, and not in me.

John Christian Perfection

GOD WILLS ALL TO BE SAVED

—

I cannot without renouncing my reason, as well as faith,
question or doubt of Thy being willing all men to be
    saved,
not only because Thou hast said it,
but also because Thou hath sent Thy only Son into the
    world, to purchase redemption and salvation
by suffering not only a weary uneasy life,
but a most painful and ignominious death for us.

Besides Thy Son Thou hast given the promise of Thy
    Spirit
that He may strengthen our decays,
purify and exalt the soul,
        by renewing and sanctifying our natures
        by illuminating our minds
        and helping us when we labour under
           infirmities.

But still strait is the gate and narrow is the way that
    leadeth unto Life
and what is yet worse there are comparatively very few
    there are that find it.

Susanna *Devotional Journal*

JESUS THE PHYSICIAN OF SOULS

—

Blessed be God, who shewed me the necessity I was in of a
Saviour to deliver me from the power of sin and Satan.
For I know that Christ will be no Saviour to such as see
    not their need of one.
You directed me by faith to lay hold of that stupendous
    mercy offered me by redeeming love.
Jesus you are the only Physician of souls,
Your blood the only salve that can heal a wounded
    conscience.

It is not in wealth, or honour, or sensual pleasure, to
    relieve a spirit heavy laden and weary of the burden
    of sin.
These things have power to increase my guilt, by
    alienating my heart from you, but none to make my
    peace with You,
to reconcile you to me, and me to you,
and to renew the union between the Divine and human
    nature.

No, there is none but Christ,
none but Christ, who is sufficient for these things.
But blessed be God, You are an all-sufficient Saviour!
Blessed be Your Holy Name, that I have found You my
    Saviour.
O I love You much, for I have much to be forgiven.

Susanna *Devotional Journal*

FOR GOD'S CONSTANT PRESENCE

—

O God, how uneasy is my mind when either company,
business or anything else diverts it from its usual course.
I have much reason to praise You.
I thank You for daily opportunities
and common mercies that are often unregarded.
So forgive and help me to see
that the more common the mercy the more valuable it
    is.
I will repeatedly acknowledge and praise You
for Your repeated acts of goodness.

When I have been for some time interrupted
in my great work and my thoughts of You have been
    diverted,
how pleasing it is to my mind
to feel the motions of Your Spirit
quickening me and exciting me to return.
But how much more delightful it is
to find a constant sense of You upon the soul.
Give me a heart whose pulse is Your praise.
This is what I chiefly endeavour to get and keep.
It will not despair for with You all things are possible!
Glory be to You!

Susanna *Devotional Journal*

TRUSTING OUR LIVES TO GOD

—

Lord I resolve by Thy Grace,
which I humbly beg
in the Name and for the sake
of the Lord Jesus,
that from this day forward,
I will resign myself and all relations
and secular concern,
to the entire management of Your good Providence.
Nor will I be anxious or solicitous
about events for the future,
in things relating only to this life.
Glory be to Thee O Lord.

Susanna *Devotional Journal*

GOD HAS NO RIVALS

—

I confess it is my duty, to love Thee my God,
with all my heart.
Give Thy strength unto Thy servant,
that Thy love may fill my heart,
and be the motive of all the use I make of my
        understanding,
my affections, my sense, my health, my time,
and whatever other talents I have received from Thee.

Let this, O God, rule my heart without a rival;
let it dispose all my thoughts, words, and works;
thus only can I fulfil my duty and Thy command,
of loving Thee with all my heart,
and mind, and soul, and strength.

John *Collection of Prayers*

DESIRING TRUE KNOWLEDGE

—

Lord,
I want the kind of knowledge of You that leads to Eternal
     Life,
not the knowledge of You that comes because I am a
     reasonable Creature.
The latter is a foreknowledge of a different kind,
which we attain in a Scientifical method by a long train
     of arguments.
It is an effect of Reason assisted by human learning,
peculiar to a few.
It makes You known only as Creator, Preserver and
     Governor of the Universe.

I want the true knowledge that comes by frequent and
     fervent application to You in prayer.
You influence and direct our reason by Your Holy Spirit.
You make Yourself known to the heart,
the will and the affections,
not merely as the Author of our own Being
but as You are exhibited to us under the character of a
     healer,
a Repairer of human nature, a Saviour him whom our
     Soul loveth.

Susanna Devotional Journal

RESTING IN GOD

—

O Lord,
I understand now that to know You only as a
    philosopher;
to have the most sublime and conscious speculations
concerning Your essence, Your attributes, Your
    providence;
to be able to demonstrate Your Being from all,
or any of the Works of nature;
and to discourse with the greatest elegancy
and propriety of words of Your existence or operations,
will avail us nothing unless at the same time we know
    You
experimentally, unless the heart perceives and knows
    You to be her Supreme Good, her only Happiness!

I know too,
that unless the Soul feels and acknowledges
that she can find no repose, no peace, no joy,
but in loving and being beloved by You;
and does accordingly rest in You as the Centre of her
    Being,
the Fountain of her pleasures, the Origin of all Virtue
    and
Goodness, her Light, her Life, her Strength, her All,
everything she wants or wisheth in this world and for
    ever in a word, her Lord, her God!

Susanna *Devotional Journal*

LOVE NOT THE WORLD

—

Your Word Lord, tells us:
>Love not the world, nor the things that are in the
>>world;
>if any man love the world,
>the love of the Father is not in him.

It is the heart you require,
help me not to fix my affections on sensual pleasures,
riches or honours, though I never enjoy any,
or a very inconsiderable proportion of them,
as he that having them all in his power,
indulges himself the satisfaction of his most criminal
>desires.

Let me not suffer my heart,
my affection to centre on any thing but you;
that the object of my passion innocent or otherwise,
might not be made my God,
that I might not forfeit my title and pretensions to
>eternal happiness.

Susanna Devotional Journal

PRACTISING GOD'S PRESENCE

—

Lord,
I want to practise a true subjection of myself to You,
not a false one as many do.
They do this for the want of consideration and
      advertence to the first principles of true religion.

Help me to be careful to avoid this inadvertence,
and to maintain a constant habitual sense of You in my
      mind.

Help me to live and act as if in Your Presence;
To think often of Your omnipotence and omniscience;
of Your power, wisdom, goodness, justice, truth,
and above all, of Your infinite purity,
which will be a check upon my mind,
and be the best preservative against all temptations.

Susanna *Devotional Journal*

A HUMBLE LIFE

—

Great and holy God, I confess, that above all others,
I have most need of humbling myself before You;
for the very great and very many sins
that I am daily guilty of,
in thought, word and deed against Your Divine Majesty.

I confess there is an habitual levity in my thoughts
and that many vain impure thoughts
pass through my mind in one hour.
Though they do not take up their abode
for any long continuance, yet their passing through,
often leaves a tincture of impurity.

Cleanse me from my secret faults.
Out of the abundance of the heart the mouth speaketh.
I am daily guilty of many vain and unnecessary words
and of neglecting the many opportunities
of speaking for the good of the souls
committed to my care.
My words as well as my thoughts are deficient.

Susanna *Devotional Journal*

ACCEPTED IN THE SON

—

Father, accept my imperfect repentance,
compassionate my infirmities,
forgive my wickedness,
purify my uncleanness,
strengthen my weakness,
fix my unstableness,
and let Thy good Spirit watch over me for ever,
and Thy love ever rule in my heart,
through the mercies and sufferings and love of Thy Son,
in whom Thou art always well pleased.

John *Collection of Prayers*

TRUE REPENTANCE

—

O Lord,
I ask that I might be possessed of that which forms the
    very essence of true repentance,
namely, the hatred and abhorrence of sin, as sin,
as it is contrary to the purity of the Divine nature and
    laws.

I know that there are excellent reasons for that hatred
    and abhorrence;
sin weakens the powers and defaces the beauty of human
    nature;
sin is attended with such mischievous consequences in
    this world and the next,
but they are not the foundation of true penitence,
for that derives its origin from a just sense of Almighty
    God,
our dependence on, and duty towards Thee as our
    Creator, Redeemer, and Sanctifier.

Susanna *Devotional Journal*

THE INTERCESSION OF THE SON

—

In mercy pass by all which Thy most pure and holy eyes
    have seen amiss in us this day.

Forgive the iniquities of our holy things;
overlook all our sins and failings,
through our great Mediator and Redeemer,
who ever lives at Thy right hand to make intercession
    for us.

And for Jesus Christ,
and for all which Thou art pleased to give us together
    with Him,
not unto us, O Lord,
but unto Thy Name be all the praise and honour and
    glory humbly ascribed by us and all Thy Church,
now and for evermore.

John *Collection of Prayers*

CERTAIN HOPE

—

Jesus to whose supreme command all things
in heaven, earth and hell submit.
Upon me lay Your mighty hand
and self shall sink beneath Your feet.
Oh let me by Your Cross abide,
You, only You, resolve to know.
The Lamb for sinners crucified,
a world to save from endless woe.

Lift up and fix my steadfast eye
on You the risen ascended Son.
On You my Head, gone up on high,
firm on Your everlasting throne.
Though earth and hell Your rule oppose,
You do as King all glorious reign.
Till Satan, sin and all Your foes,
and death, the last of all, be slain.

Charles *Hymns and Poems*

HE IS OUR HOPE

—

Come, O my Hope, my Life, my Lord
and fix in me your lasting home.
Be mindful of your gracious Word
and with your promised Father come.
Prepare and then possess my heart.
Oh take me, seize me from above.
You do I love, for God you are.
You do I feel, for God is love.

Charles *Hymns and Poems*

FILLED WITH HOPE

—

Jesus, Your feeble servant fill
with power
            to labour up the hill,
with zeal
            toward the high prize to press,
with violent faith
            the crown to seize.
By You stirred up, I'll strive again.
I'll after full perfection strain,
instant in prayer's strong agony,
till pure in heart Your face I see.

Then, then my soul with rapid speed
shall labour up to grasp its Head.
All vigour, all activity, I live,
not I but Christ in me.
Passive, yet swift as light I fly,
filled with the Power that fills the sky.
And draws me to that glorious throne,
to live with You for ever one.

Charles Hymns and Poems

HOPE OF FINAL RESTORATION

—

Jesus shall I never be firmly grounded upon you?
Steadfastly behold your face, established with abiding
    grace?
Oh how wavering is my mind, tossed about with every
    wind!
Oh how quickly does my heart from my living God
    depart!

Easily I fall away, never am I at one stay.
Strong in faith I seem this hour,
stripped the next of all my power.
Seek, oh seek me, Lord, again.
Comfort to my soul restore.
Come and never leave me more.

Charles *Hymns and Poems*

TEACH ME TO PRAY

—

O that the power were mine, to saints and prophets
    given.
The power of faithful prayer divine, which shuts and
    opens heaven.
Then would I wrestle on and more than conqueror prove,
and bring the hallowing Spirit down in showers of purest
    love.

Your servant Lord, prepare, your glory to display.
Remove this unbelieving bar and teach me how to pray.
Author of faith you are,
help my infirmity and put your Spirit within my heart
    and pray yourself in me.

Charles Hymns and Poems

DO I REALLY PRAY?

—

Have I prayed with fervour?
At going in and out of Church?
In the Church?
Morning and evening in private?
Monday, Wednesday, and Friday, with my friends, at
    rising?
Before lying down?
On Saturday noon?
All the time I am engaged in exterior work in private?
Before I go into the place of public or private prayer,
for help therein?

Have I, wherever I was, gone to Church morning and
    evening,
unless for necessary mercy?
And spent from one hour to three in private?
Have I, in private prayer,
frequently stopped short and observed what fervour?

Have I repeated it over and over,
till I adverted to every word?
Have I at the beginning of every prayer or paragraph
    owned I cannot pray?

John 'Self-Examination'

THE SPIRIT OF PRAYER

—

You Lord, have given the wish to pray,
the longing wish which now I feel.
But oh I know not what to say.
I would, but cannot, Lord,
reveal the load my fainting spirits bear,
or tell you all my wants in prayer.

Do you not Lord, my trouble see,
my sore, unprofitable pain?
A thousand times I bow the knee,
approach you with my lips in vain.
Present with lifted hands and eyes,
a heartless, lifeless sacrifice.

A thousand times overwhelmed with woe,
I groan impatient at your stay,
ready to let the promise go,
ready to cast my shield away.
The fruitless labour to forbear
and fold my arms in sad despair.

Jesus regard your supplicant,
your needy, tempted follower here.
And now supply my desperate want
and send me down the Comforter.
The Spirit of ceaseless prayer impart
and fix your Agent in my heart.

Charles *Hymns and Poems*

A LIFE OF PRAYER

God's command, to pray without ceasing,
is founded on the necessity we have of his grace,
to preserve the life of God in the soul,
which can no more subsist one moment without it
than the body can without air.

Whether we think of or speak to God,
whether we act or suffer for him,
all is prayer,
when we have no other object than his love,
and the desire of pleasing Him.

All that a Christian does,
even in eating and sleeping is prayer,
when it is done in simplicity,
according to the order of God,
without either adding to or diminishing from it
by his own choice.

John *Christian Perfection*

PERFECT PRAYER

—

Prayer continues in the desire of the heart,
tho' the understanding be employed on outward things.
In souls filled with love,
the desire to please God is a continual prayer.

As the furious hate which the devil bears us is termed
    the roaring of the lion,
so our vehement love may be termed crying after God.

God only requires of his adult children that their hearts
    be truly purified,
and that they offer him continually the wishes and vows
    that naturally spring from perfect love.

For these desires,
being the genuine fruits of love,
are the most perfect prayers that can spring from it.

John *Christian Perfection*

PREPARATION FOR PRAYER

—

Enable me, O God,
to collect and compose my thoughts before an immediate
    approach to You in prayer.
May I be careful to have my mind in order
when I take upon myself the honour
to speak to the Sovereign Lord of the Universe,
remembering that upon the temper of my soul depends,
in very great measure, my success.

You are infinitely too great to be trifled with.
Too wise to be imposed on by a mock devotion and abhor
    a sacrifice without a heart.
Help me to entertain an habitual sense of Your
    perfections,
as an admirable help against cold and formal
    performances.

Save me from engaging in rash and precipitate prayers
    and from abrupt breaking away
to follow business or pleasure as though I had never
    prayed.

Susanna *Devotional Journal*

GIVING ONESELF TO GOD

—

I give Thee my understanding:
may it be my only care to know Thee,
Thy perfections, Thy works, and Thy will.

I give Thee my will.
May I have no will of my own.
Whatsoever Thou willest
may I will and that only.
May I will Thy glory
in all things as Thou dost,
and make that my end in everything.

I give Thee my affections.
Do Thou dispose of them all.
Be Thou my love, my fear, my joy.
And may nothing have any share in them
but with respect to Thee and for Thy sake.

What Thou lovest may I love;
what Thou hatest may I hate;
and that in such measure
as Thou art pleased to prescribe me.

I give Thee my body.
May I glorify Thee with it
and preserve it holy,
fit for Thee, O God, to dwell in.
May I neither indulge it
nor use too much rigour toward it,
but keep it, as far as in me lies,
healthy, vigorous, and active,
and fit to do Thee in all manner of service,
which Thou shalt call for.

I give Thee all my worldly goods.
May I prize them and use them only for Thee.
May I faithfully restore to Thee, in Thy poor,
all Thou hast entrusted me with,
above the necessaries of my life,
and be content to part with them too,
whenever Thou, my Lord,
shalt require them at my hands.

I give Thee my credit and reputation.
May I never value them
but only in respect of Thee;
nor endeavour to maintain them
but as they may do Thee service
and advance Thy honour in the world.

I give Thee myself and my all
Let me look upon myself to be nothing,
and to have nothing, out of Thee.
Be Thou the sole disposer
and governor of myself and all I have.
Be Thou my portion and my all.

O my God and my all, when hereafter
I shall be tempted to break this solemn engagement,
when I shall be prest to conform to the world,
and to the company and customs that surround me,
may my answer be: I am not my own.
I am not for myself,
nor for the world, but for my God.
I will give unto God the things which are God's.
God be merciful to me a sinner.

John *Collection of Prayers*

PRESSING ONWARD

—

Lord help me never take up my rest on this side of
    heaven,
nor think I have enough of you,
till I am perfectly renewed and sanctified
in body, soul and spirit;
till I am admitted into that blessed region
of pure and happy spirits,
where I shall enjoy the beatific vision
according to the measure of my capacity!

Susanna Devotional Journal

DESIRING TO PLEASE GOD

—

Help me Lord, to do the main thing, to endeavour all I
    can,
to be assured that I love You,
which assurance can no way be attained but by the
    evidence of a good life.

That my mind should habitually press after a conformity
    to Your Divine will,
and should in all its actions chiefly desire to please and
    approve itself to You,
and this without regarding the world,
or the favour or displeasure of men any further than
    Your honour and glory is concerned.

That I should have an habitual tendency and desire of
    union and
enjoyment of You, and in all circumstances, places, and
    times,
preserve a habit of submission and entire resignation to
    the order of Your providence.

Both when it crosses our worldly interest,
and prevents our best laid designs and contrivances for
    the advancement of Your glory, as when it favours
    them.

Susanna *Devotional Journal*

BEING ZEALOUS

—

O God, fill my soul with so entire a love of Thee that I
    may love nothing
but for Thy sake and in subordination to Thy love.

Give me grace to study Thy knowledge daily,
that the more I know Thee,
the more I may love Thee.

Create in me a zealous obedience to all Thy commands,
a cheerful patience under all Thy chastisements,
and a thankful resignation to all Thy disposals.

Let it be the one business of my life to glorify Thee,
by every word of my tongue, by every work of my
    hand;
by professing Thy truth, and by engaging all men,
so far as in me lies, to glorify and love Thee.

John *Collection of Prayers*

GOD DESERVES OUR WORSHIP AND SERVICE

—

You are a Great and All Glorious God from Whom we
    received our being and whatever we have
that does in any way render that being pleasing to
    ourselves or useful to others.
The inference is very just that a God of such Immense
    Perfection, hath a just Right to our Worship and
    Service,
which is the foundation of all practical Religion.

But how to worship and serve You after an acceptable
    manner is the Grand Enquiry.
To that end we ought to use the greatest application and
    seriousness,
because our present and eternal Happiness depends on a
    conformity to Your Will, our Great Creator.
Now in order to do Your will, it is necessary that we
    should know it.

But we could not know it in our present state, had it not
pleased You, Almighty God, to reveal Your Will unto
    us.
What You would have us believe and do,
that we may so please and honour You, as to enjoy Your
    Favour.
The consequence of which is Eternal Happiness.

Susanna *Devotional Journal*

THE DESIRE TO SERVE GOD

—

Though with my mind, my judgment
and intellectual powers I serve Your Law,
and do truly, in my sober reflections
always prefer You and Your service
before all sensual enjoyments whatever;
yet I often perceive
that I have too great a regard
for the ease and pleasures of this wretched body;
am too careful to provide its necessaries,
too much afraid of injuring it,
too indulgent to its appetites,
and in all things too solicitous for its welfare
and continuance in this life.

Susanna *Devotional Journal*

JESUS IS OUR PATTERN

—

I commit my soul morning and evening
to Jesus Christ
as he is the Saviour of the world.
Help me, O God,
to observe what he saith unto me;
resolutely to obey his precepts
and to endeavour to follow his example
in those things wherein
he is exhibited to us
as a pattern for our imitation.

No circumstances or time of life
can occur but I may find
something either spoken by my Lord himself
or by His Spirit in the Prophets or Apostles,
that will direct my conduct
if I am but faithful to You and my own soul.

Susanna *Devotional Journal*

THE NEED FOR GOD'S STRENGTH

—

Oh God,
Thou knowest that Light without Strength
is not sufficient for me;
since it will only put me
in the number of those unprofitable servants
that knew their Master's will and did it not.
Vouchsafe for the sake of the Lord Jesus,
to give me strength and a disposition of heart,
to obey the dictates of Thy Good Spirit.
Amen.

Susanna Devotional Journal

THE COMMAND TO INTERCEDE

—

Holy, holy, holy, Lord God Almighty,
I, miserable sinner, humbly acknowledge that I am
    altogether unworthy to pray for myself.
But since You have commanded me to make prayers and
intercessions for all men,
in obedience to Your command,
and confidence of Your unlimited goodness,
I commend to Your mercy the wants and necessities of
    all mankind.

John Collection of Prayers

FOR THE BRETHREN

—

Let no temptation expose me to ingratitude
or make me forfeit Thy loving-kindness
which is better than life itself.
But grant that I may assist all my brethren
with my prayers where I cannot reach them
with actual services.
Make me zealous to embrace all occasions
that may minister to their happiness.
Let Thy love to me
be the pattern of my love to them.

John *Collection of Prayers*

THE NEEDS OF OTHERS

—

Be gracious to all who are near and dear to me.
Thou knowest their names and art acquainted with their
    wants.
Of Thy goodness be pleased to proportion Thy blessings
to their necessities.

Pardon my enemies, and give them repentance and
    charity,
and me grace to overcome evil with good.
Have compassion on all who are distressed
in mind, body, or estate;
give them steady patience and timely deliverance.

John *Collection of Prayers*

SPIRIT OF INTERCESSION

—

Spirit of interceding grace,
I know not how or what to pray.
Assist my utter helplessness,
the power into my heart convey.
That God, acknowledging your groan,
may answer in my prayers His own.

Charles *Hymns and Poems*

THE STILL, SMALL VOICE

—

Gracious God, what an exceeding condescension it is
for Your Holy Spirit at any time to vouchsafe
His assistance to such a sinful,
worthless creature as I am!
Help me to be careful lest at any time
I should grieve You and provoke You to depart from me.
For as You have said,
        'My Spirit shall not always strive with man'.

By grace I stand.
Let me not despise or neglect this grace.
Help me to be extremely careful
to purify my mind from all that may offend You
and as much as possible, separate from the world.
The still, small voice is not heard
amidst the thunder and noise of tumultuous passions.
Keep my mind in a temper for recollection.
Often in the day,
help me to call it in from outward objects,
lest it wander into forbidden paths.

Susanna *Devotional Journal*

THE WELL OF LIFE

—

You promised to impart Yourself
to all who ask Yourself of You.
Open the fountain in my heart,
spring up, O Well of life in me.
The Root and Principle of grace
in me let Your good Spirit abide.
Renew in perfect holiness
and add me to the glorified.

Not like a sudden transient flood
but fixed and permanent and sure.
The grace You have on me bestowed
deep let it in my soul endure.
Swift to its source celestial move,
freely fulfil your whole design
with all the activity of love,
with all the powers of life divine.

Charles *Hymns and Poems*

THE SPIRIT OF THE SON

———

Send forth the Spirit of your Son, O God, into my
    longing heart.
That governed by your love alone, from you I never may
    depart.
But following my celestial Guide, be numbered with the
    glorified.

Charles *Hymns and Poems*

PRAYERS
FOR OTHERS

Friends, Family and Relations – Travellers –
The Sick and Dying – The Church –
Missionaries – The Nation

THE FATHER'S PROTECTION

—

O my God,
I praise Thee for Thy continual preservation of me,
for Thy fatherly protection over me this day,
for all the comforts with which Thou hast surrounded
    me,
spiritual and temporal,
particularly for leave now to pray unto Thee.

Accept my poor services;
pardon the sinfulness of this and all my holy duties;
and bless me, my friends and relations,
my benefactors and mine enemies,
this night and for ever, with the blessings of Thy
    children.

John *Collection of Prayers*

THE BEST BLESSING

—

Be gracious to all our friends and neighbours.
Bless our relations with the best of Thy blessings,
with Thy fear and love.
Preserve us from our enemies,
and reconcile them both to us and to Thyself.

John *Collection of Prayers*

A FAITHFUL FAMILY

—

O That all the habitations of Christians
may be the houses of prayer!
Let Thy blessing rest upon us of this family.
In every condition secure our hearts to Thyself,
and make us ever to approve ourselves sincere and
   faithful in Thy service.

John *Collection of Prayers*

—

BENEDICTION

—

I heartily pray God that you may continue steadfast in
    the faith,
and increase more and more in the knowledge and love
    of God,
and of His Son Jesus Christ.
That Holiness, simplicity, and purity may recommend
    you to the favour of God incarnate.
That His Spirit may dwell in you, and keep you still, as now,
under a sense of God's blissful presence.

Susanna *Devotional Journal*

THAT GOD WILL VISIT

—

Shower down Thy graces on all my relations,
on all my friends and all that belong to this family.
Comfort and relieve those that labour under any
    difficulties of body or mind;
especially those who suffer for the testimony of a good
    conscience.
Visit them, O gracious Lord, in all their distresses.
Thou knowest, Thou seest them under all.
O stay their souls upon Thee.

And grant us all, together with Thy whole Church,
an entrance into Thine everlasting Kingdom,
through Jesus Christ, to whom with Thee and the
    blessed Spirit,
Three Persons and One God, be ascribed all majesty,
dominion, and power, now and for evermore.

John *Collection of Prayers*

PRAYING IN UNITY

—

Be gracious to my relations,
to all that are endeared to me
by their kindnesses and acquaintance,
to all who remember me in their prayers
or desire to be remembered in mine.

Sanctify, O merciful Lord,
the friendship which Thou hast granted me
with these Thy servants.
Let our prayers be heard for each other,
while our hearts are united in Thy fear and love,
and graciously unite them therein more and more.

Strengthen our hearts
against all corruptions and temptations.
Enable us to consecrate ourselves
faithfully and entirely to Thy service.
Grant that we may provoke each other
to love and serve Thee,
and grow up together before Thee
in Thy fear and love, to Thy heavenly Kingdom.

And by Thy infinite mercies vouchsafe to bring us,
with those that are dead in Thee,
to rejoice together before Thee,
through the merits of our Lord Jesus Christ,
to whom with Thee and the Holy Ghost,
the blessed and only Potentate,
the King of Kings and Lord of Lords,
be honour and power everlasting.

John *Collection of Prayers*

TRAVELLING WITH GOD

—

Extend, O Lord,
Thy pity to the whole race of mankind.
Be merciful to all that are in distress,
that struggle with pain, poverty or reproach.
Be Thou a guide to them that travel by land or by water.

John Collection of Prayers

FOR THE HURTING ONES

—

Preserve my parents,
my brothers and sisters,
friends and relations,
and all mankind,
in their souls and bodies.

Forgive mine enemies and in Thy due time make them
    kindly affectioned toward me.
Have mercy on all who are afflicted in mind, body, or
    estate.
Give them patience under their sufferings,
and a happy issue out of all their afflictions.

O grant that we,
with those who are already dead in Thy faith and fear,
may together partake of a joyful resurrection,
through Him who liveth and reigneth with Thee and the
    Holy Ghost,
one God, world without end.

John *Collection of Prayers*

GOD'S SPECIAL CONCERN

—

Give Thy grace, O holy Jesus, to all the world,
and let all who are redeemed by Thy blood acknowledge
    Thee to be the Lord.
Let all Christians, especially those of this nation,
keep themselves unspotted from the world.

Be a help at hand to all that are afflicted and assist them
    to trust in Thee.
Raise up friends for the widow and fatherless,
the friendless and oppressed.

Give patience to all that are sick,
comfort to all troubled consciences,
strength to all that are tempted.

John *Collection of Prayers*

GOD OF COMFORT

—

Strengthen all Thy faithful servants.
Bring back them that wander out of the way.
Raise up those that are fallen.
Confirm those that stand,
and grant them steadily to persevere
in faith, love, and obedience.
Relieve and comfort all that are in distress.

Let the earth bring forth her fruit in due season,
and let all honest and industrious people
be blest in their labours.
Remember all those who have done good unto us.
Grant forgiveness and charity to all our enemies,
and continue goodwill among all our neighbours.

Support the sick with faith and patience.
Assist those who are leaving this world.
Receive the souls which Thou hast redeemed
with Thy Son's precious blood,
and sanctified by the Holy Spirit,
and give us all a glorious resurrection and eternal life.

John *Collection of Prayers*

GOD'S CHURCH

—

Bless, O gracious Father,
all the nations whom Thou hast placed upon the earth,
with the knowledge of Thee, the only true God:
but especially bless Thy holy catholic Church and fill it
    with truth and grace.

Where it is corrupt, purge it;
Where it is in error, rectify it;
Where it is right, confirm it;
Where it is divided and rent asunder,
    heal the breaches thereof.

Replenish all whom Thou hast called to any office
    therein,
with truth of doctrine and innocency of life.
Let their prayers be as precious incense in Thy sight,
that their cries and tears for the City of God may not be
    in vain.

John *Collection of Prayers*

A SPIRITUAL CHURCH

—

Hear also my prayers for all mankind,
and guide their feet into the way of peace:
For Thy holy catholic Church,
let her live by Thy Spirit
and reign in Thy glory.
Remember that branch of it
which Thou hast planted in these Kingdoms,
especially the stewards of Thy holy mysteries.
Give them such zeal, diligence and wisdom,
that they may save both themselves
and those that hear them.

John *Collection of Prayers*

A WISE CHURCH

—

Thou great Shepherd of souls,
bring home into Thy fold all that are gone astray.
Preserve Thy Church from all heresy and schism,
from all that persecute or oppose the truth;
and give unto Thy ministers wisdom and holiness
and the powerful aid of Thy blessed Spirit.

John *Collection of Prayers*

A PEACEFUL CHURCH

—

Hear the daily prayers of the catholic Church.
Free her from error.
Let the truth as it is in Jesus prevail,
and peace be in all her borders.

John *Collection of Prayers*

A PRAYING CHURCH

—

O God, who by Thy Holy Spirit
didst at first establish a Church,
and who, sanctifying it by the same Spirit,
still preserve and govern it;
hear, we beseech Thee,
the prayers of Thy servants,
and mercifully grant us
the perpetual assistance of Thy grace.

That we may never be deceived
by any false spirit,
nor overcome by the suggestions
of flesh and blood,
but in all our doubts
may be directed in the ways of truth,
and in all our actions
guided by this Thy Holy Spirit.
Who, with Thee, and Thy eternal Son,
liveth and reigneth,
one God, world without end.

John *Collection of Prayers*

PROSPER YOUR SERVANTS

—

Let the prayers and sacrifices of Thy holy Church
offered unto Thee this day,
be graciously accepted.
Clothe Thy priests with righteousness,
and pardon all Thy people who are not prepared
according to the preparation of the sanctuary.

Prosper all those who are sincerely engaged in
     propagating or promoting Thy faith and love.
Give Thy Son the heathen for His inheritance,
and the uttermost parts of the earth for His possession,
that from the rising up of the sun
unto the going down of the same,
Thy Name may be great among the Gentiles.

John *Collection of Prayers*

TURN AGAIN LORD

—

Have mercy upon this Kingdom
and forgive the sins of this people.
Turn Thee unto us, bless us,
and cause Thy face to shine on our desolations.

John Collection of Prayers

KING OF KINGS

—

Be gracious to this our native land.
Do Thou rule all our rulers,
counsel all our counsellors,
teach all our teachers,
and order all the public affairs to Thy glory.

Turn from us the judgments which we feel or fear.
Continue Thy blessings to our souls and bodies.
And notwithstanding all our provocations,
be Thou still our God and let us be Thy people.

John Collection of Prayers

Abbreviations

—

Banner

The Wesley Banner, July–December 1852: a series of anonymous articles that appeared in this short-lived periodical, entitled 'Journal of Mrs Susanna Wesley'. The bulk of the entries are verbatim transcripts of selections from the *Manuscripts of Susanna Wesley*, now held at Wesley College, Bristol.

Christian Perfection

A Plain Account of Christian Perfection (2nd edn 1766), as contained within Wesley's *Collected Works* (see below), vol. 11.

Clarke

Adam Clarke, *Memoirs of the Wesley Family* (London 1823).

Collection

These prayers are from the writings entitled *A Collection of Forms of Prayer for Every Day of the Week* (1733); *A Collection of Prayers for Families*; and *Devotions for Every Day of the Week*. The editions used are those contained in Wesley's *Collected Works* (see below), vol. 11.

'Covenant Service'

Wesley's 'Covenant Service' (1780), as included in Wesley's *Collected Works* (see below).

MSS

Selections taken direct from the *Manuscripts* that contain the writings of Susanna Wesley. The selections used come mainly from the *Devotional Journal of Susanna Wesley*.

The *Manuscripts* include 'Meditations and Reflexions by Mrs Susanna Wesley' (Manuscript D2/2).

A *Notebook* containing 192 pages of meditational entries numbered from the front, and a further 19 pages of entries numbered from the rear of the *Notebook*.

Susanna has dated the title page with the year 1709 (D2/3).

The third *Manuscript* contains three long letters written by Susanna to her son Samuel and daughter Susanna.

There are thirty further pages of her *Devotional Journal* at the rear of the *Notebook* (D2/6).

Poetical Works

These refer to selections taken from *The Poetical Works of John and Charles Wesley*, 1868–72. This is a thirteen-volume series of writings which contains hymns written mainly by both brothers, but predominantly by Charles, on a wide variety of subjects.

'Self-Examination'

The writings of John Wesley, as found in his *Collected Works* (see below).

Works

The Collected Works of John Wesley, in seventeen volumes (London 1812).

Further Reading

—

J. A. Newton, *Susanna Wesley and the Puritan Tradition in Methodism* (London, Epworth 1968).

C. Wallace, Jr, 'Susanna Wesley's Spirituality: The Freedom of a Christian Woman', *Methodist History*, 22: 3 (April 1984).

'Journal of Mrs Susanna Wesley', anonymous series of articles, *The Wesley Banner* (July–December 1852).

A. Clarke, *Memoirs of the Wesley Family* (London, 1823).

J. Whitehead, *Life of Wesley* (1793).

W. L. Doughty, *The Prayers of Susanna Wesley* (London, Epworth 1956).

The Collected Works of John Wesley various editions.

J. and C. Wesley, *The Poetical Works* (London, 1868–72).

J. A. Kay, *Wesley's Prayers and Praises* (London, Epworth 1958).

Notes and Sources

Page no.

3 Clarke, p. 312.

4 Clarke, p. 326.

5 MSS D2/2, p. 24. Susanna dated this meditation 1 March 1710.
Poetical Works, vol. 9, p. 174.

6 *Poetical Works*, vol. 4, p. 34.

7 *Banner*, p. 248.

8–9 MSS D2/3, p. 9.

9 *Collection*, p. 294.

10 *Collection*, p. 283.

11 MSS D2/2, p. 36.

12 *Banner*, p. 246.

13 *Collection*, p. 286.

14 *Poetical Works*, vol. 11, p. 503.

15 MSS D2/3, p. 17.

16 *Christian Perfection*, p. 241.

17 MSS D2/3, p. 7.

18 Clarke, p. 324.

19 *Collection*, p. 285.

20 *Collection*, p. 339.
Collection, p. 316.

21 *Collection*, p. 329.

22 *Collection*, p. 332.

23 *Collection*, p. 295.

24 *Collection*, pp. 307–8.
Collection, p. 313.

25 *Collection*, p. 319.

26 *Collection*, p. 334.

27 *Collection*, p. 359.
Collection, p. 359.

28 MSS D2/3, p. 24.

29 MSS D2/3, p. 2.

30 MSS D2/3, p. 8.

33–9 MSS D2/3, p. 13.

35 MSS D2/4, p. 49.

36–7 *Collection*, p. 278.

38 MSS D2/3, p. 55.

39 *Banner*, p. 247.
MSS D2/2, p. 9.

40 Clarke, p. 280. This prayer of praise is to be found in a letter written by Susanna to her son John on 27 November 1735. The letter concerns the happiness she experienced as a result of her close and constant communion with God. The joy of the letter is put into context when one realizes that she had only a few months before buried the husband she had been married to since the age of twenty. The letter was written while she was visiting her daughter Emily in Gainsborough.

41–2 Clarke, pp. 290–1.

43 'Covenant Service'.

44 *Poetical Works*, vol. 2, p. 277.

45 *Banner*, p. 247.

46 *Collection*, p. 312.

47 MSS D2/4, p. 4.

48–9 MSS D2/4, p. 9.

50 MSS D2/4, p. 20.

51 MSS D2/4, p. 21.

52 MSS D2/4, p. 57.

53 'Covenant Service'.

54 *Collection*, p. 290.

55 *Collection*, p. 293.

56 *Collection*, p. 299.

57 *Collection*, pp. 309–10.

58–9 *Poetical Works*, vol. 1, pp. 76–9.

60 *Poetical Works*, vol. 10, p. 143.

61 *Christian Perfection*, p. 241.

62 MSS D2/3, p. 9.

63 Clarke, p. 346.

64 MSS D2/3, p. 58.

65 MSS D2/3, p. 20. Entry written on the morning of 29 January 1723.

66 *Collection*, p. 280.

67 MSS D2/3, p. 6.

68 MSS D2/2, p. 7.

69 Clarke, p. 320.

70 MSS D2/3, p. 33.

71 MSS D2/3, p. 55.

72 *Collection*, p. 311.

73 *Banner*, p. 247.

74 *Collection*, p. 342.

75 *Poetical Works*, vol. 2, p. 332.

76 *Poetical Works*, vol. 1, p. 75.

77 *Poetical Works*, vol. 13, p. 126.